FIRST GRADE GEOGRAPHY RIVERS AND LAKES OF THE WORLD

Speedy Publishing LLC
40 E. Main St. #1156
Newark, DE 19711
www.speedypublishing.com

Some rivers form
when lakes overflow.

A river is
freshwater
flowing across
the surface of
the land, usually
to the sea.

Rivers flow in channels. The bottom of the channel is called the bed and the sides of the channel are called the banks.

Water from
a river can
come from rain,
melting snow,
lakes, ponds, or
even glaciers.

Lakes are
large bodies
of water that
are surrounded
by land and
are not part of
an ocean.

A lake usually contains freshwater but some can be saltwater.

Lakes form when water finds its way into a basin. Lakes must have a continual source of new water, otherwise they will eventually dry up.

Most lakes
only last a
few thousand
years and then
disappear.